Clarence™
MAD LIBS®

by Brian Elling

PSS!
PRICE STERN SLOAN
An Imprint of Penguin Random House

PRICE STERN SLOAN
Penguin Young Readers Group
An Imprint of Penguin Random House LLC

Concept created by Roger Price & Leonard Stern

Published by Price Stern Sloan, an imprint of Penguin Random House LLC,
345 Hudson Street, New York, New York 10014.
Printed in the USA.

ISBN 978-0-8431-8337-5
1 3 5 7 9 10 8 6 4 2

MAD●LIBS®

INSTRUCTIONS

MAD LIBS® is a game for people who don't like games! It can be played by one, two, three, four, or forty.

• RIDICULOUSLY SIMPLE DIRECTIONS

In this tablet you will find stories containing blank spaces where words are left out. One player, the READER, selects one of these stories. The READER does not tell anyone what the story is about. Instead, he/she asks the other players, the WRITERS, to give him/her words. These words are used to fill in the blank spaces in the story.

• TO PLAY

The READER asks each WRITER in turn to call out a word—an adjective or a noun or whatever the space calls for—and uses them to fill in the blank spaces in the story. The result is a MAD LIBS® game.

When the READER then reads the completed MAD LIBS® game to the other players, they will discover that they have written a story that is fantastic, screamingly funny, shocking, silly, crazy, or just plain dumb—depending upon which words each WRITER called out.

• EXAMPLE (*Before* and *After*)

" _____ !" he said _____
    EXCLAMATION   ADVERB

as he jumped into his convertible _____ and
                                              NOUN

drove off with his _____ wife.
                        ADJECTIVE

" _____*Ouch*_____ !" he said _____*stupidly*_____
    EXCLAMATION   ADVERB

as he jumped into his convertible _____*cat*_____ and
                                              NOUN

drove off with his _____*brave*_____ wife.
                        ADJECTIVE

MAD LIBS
QUICK REVIEW

In case you have forgotten what adjectives, adverbs, nouns, and verbs are, here is a quick review:

An ADJECTIVE describes something or somebody. *Lumpy, soft, ugly, messy,* and *short* are adjectives.

An ADVERB tells how something is done. It modifies a verb and usually ends in "ly." *Modestly, stupidly, greedily,* and *carefully* are adverbs.

A NOUN is the name of a person, place, or thing. *Sidewalk, umbrella, bridle, bathtub,* and *nose* are nouns.

A VERB is an action word. *Run, pitch, jump,* and *swim* are verbs. Put the verbs in past tense if the directions say PAST TENSE. *Ran, pitched, jumped,* and *swam* are verbs in the past tense.

When we ask for A PLACE, we mean any sort of place: a country or city (*Spain, Cleveland*) or a room (*bathroom, kitchen*).

An EXCLAMATION or SILLY WORD is any sort of funny sound, gasp, grunt, or outcry, like *Wow!, Ouch!, Whomp!, Ick!,* and *Gadzooks!*

When we ask for specific words, like a NUMBER, a COLOR, an ANIMAL, or a PART OF THE BODY, we mean a word that is one of those things, like *seven, blue, horse,* or *head.*

When we ask for a PLURAL, it means more than one. For example, *cat* pluralized is *cats.*

MAD LIBS® is fun to play with friends, but you can also play it by yourself! To begin with, DO NOT look at the story on the page below. Fill in the blanks on this page with the words called for. Then, using the words you have selected, fill in the blank spaces in the story.

Now you've created your own hilarious MAD LIBS® game!

THE BEST OF FRIENDS

ADJECTIVE _____

VERB _____

NOUN _____

ADJECTIVE _____

NOUN _____

NOUN _____

PART OF THE BODY _____

OCCUPATION _____

NOUN _____

ADJECTIVE _____

ADVERB _____

PERSON IN ROOM _____

TYPE OF FOOD (PLURAL) _____

NOUN _____

ADJECTIVE _____

PLURAL NOUN _____

MAD LIBS

THE BEST OF FRIENDS

Clarence loves to spend time with Jeff and Sumo, his _____
ADJECTIVE

friends! He'd rather _____ with them than anybody else
VERB

in the whole wide _____. But these three friends couldn't
NOUN

be more _____. Jeff loves cleaning his _____
ADJECTIVE   NOUN

and has a head shaped like a/an _____. On the other
NOUN

_____, Sumo loves adventure, is a dare-_____,
PART OF THE BODY   OCCUPATION

and has no _____ on his head at all! And Clarence just
NOUN

likes to have a ton of _____ fun. Given how different
ADJECTIVE

these three are, who would ever imagine that they would get along

so _____? But Jeff, Sumo, and _____ are like
ADVERB   PERSON IN ROOM

three _____ in a pod who have been permanently stuck
TYPE OF FOOD (PLURAL)

together with super-_____. Maybe that _____
NOUN   ADJECTIVE

saying " _____ attract" is true after all!
PLURAL NOUN

MAD LIBS® is fun to play with friends, but you can also play it by yourself! To begin with, DO NOT look at the story on the page below. Fill in the blanks on this page with the words called for. Then, using the words you have selected, fill in the blank spaces in the story.

Now you've created your own hilarious MAD LIBS® game!

HOME, SWEET ABERDALE

ADJECTIVE _____

NOUN _____

ADJECTIVE _____

TYPE OF FOOD _____

PERSON IN ROOM (FEMALE) _____

VERB ENDING IN "ING" _____

NOUN _____

NOUN _____

TYPE OF FOOD (PLURAL) _____

VERB _____

ANIMAL _____

OCCUPATION _____

ADJECTIVE _____

VERB _____

NOUN _____

NOUN _____

EXCLAMATION _____

MAD LIBS®

HOME, SWEET ABERDALE

Aberdale is such a/an _____ place to live! This town has
_____ADJECTIVE_____

everything that a/an _____ like Clarence could want—and
_____NOUN_____

more! It has _____ restaurants, like the _____
_____ADJECTIVE_____   _____TYPE OF FOOD_____

Shack (where Clarence had his first date with _____),
_____PERSON IN ROOM (FEMALE)_____

and restaurants for family _____, like Chuckleton's—
_____VERB ENDING IN "ING"_____

"where the _____ tastes funny!" The Aberdale Zoo is a perfect
_____NOUN_____

place for a field _____. Just be careful if you're allergic to
_____NOUN_____

_____, because the elephants _____ peanuts
__TYPE OF FOOD (PLURAL)__   _____VERB_____

all day long! The zoo is also where Clarence saw a baby _____
_____ANIMAL_____

swimming with its _____! That was so _____!
_____OCCUPATION_____   _____ADJECTIVE_____

But no visit to Aberdale would be complete without taking time to

_____ for a few minutes in Bendle Park. Who knows? You
_____VERB_____

might even see an erratic _____ while you're there, which is
_____NOUN_____

a big _____ left behind by glaciers. _____!
_____NOUN_____   _____EXCLAMATION_____

MAD LIBS® is fun to play with friends, but you can also play it by yourself! To begin with, DO NOT look at the story on the page below. Fill in the blanks on this page with the words called for. Then, using the words you have selected, fill in the blank spaces in the story.

Now you've created your own hilarious MAD LIBS® game!

MS. BAKER'S CLASSROOM RULES OF CONDUCT

ADJECTIVE _____

COLOR _____

PLURAL NOUN _____

PART OF THE BODY (PLURAL) _____

VERB _____

ANIMAL (PLURAL) _____

VERB _____

PLURAL NOUN _____

TYPE OF FOOD _____

ADJECTIVE _____

ADJECTIVE _____

A PLACE _____

VERB _____

PLURAL NOUN _____

LETTER OF THE ALPHABET _____

PERSON IN ROOM _____

MAD LIBS®
MS. BAKER'S CLASSROOM
RULES OF CONDUCT

Here's a list of _____ rules that Ms. Baker wrote on the
_____ ADJECTIVE

_____-board in her classroom:
COLOR

1. Do not put _____ in your _____,
PLURAL NOUN   PART OF THE BODY (PLURAL)

   even if you will look like a walrus when you _____
VERB

   around on the floor. No pencil _____ in class!
ANIMAL (PLURAL)

2. Do not _____ your Buddy _____, even if
VERB   PLURAL NOUN

   the glue tastes like _____. _____ Stars are
TYPE OF FOOD   ADJECTIVE

   not food!

3. Do not pass out invitations to _____ parties while
ADJECTIVE

   in (the) _____. If you do, students who you did not
A PLACE

   _____ might get their _____ hurt.
VERB   PLURAL NOUN

4. Do not ask the teacher to change your grade from a/an

   _____ to an A just so you can be in the Quill
LETTER OF THE ALPHABET

   group. This means you, _____!
PERSON IN ROOM

From CLARENCE MAD LIBS® • TM & © Cartoon Network (s16). Published by Price Stern Sloan,
an imprint of Penguin Random House LLC, 345 Hudson Street, New York, NY 10014.

MAD LIBS® is fun to play with friends, but you can also play it by yourself! To begin with, DO NOT look at the story on the page below. Fill in the blanks on this page with the words called for. Then, using the words you have selected, fill in the blank spaces in the story.

Now you've created your own hilarious MAD LIBS® game!

SUMO'S DREAM BOAT

NOUN _____

VERB ENDING IN "ING" _____

PART OF THE BODY _____

NOUN _____

VERB _____

PLURAL NOUN _____

ADJECTIVE _____

NOUN _____

COLOR _____

ANIMAL _____

NUMBER _____

TYPE OF LIQUID _____

ADJECTIVE _____

ADJECTIVE _____

VERB _____

SAME VERB _____

ADVERB _____

VERB ENDING IN "ING" _____

MAD LIBS

SUMO'S DREAM BOAT

Sumo's goal in life was to build his very own dream _____.
NOUN

But _____ his boat turned out to be harder than he
VERB ENDING IN "ING"

thought. It took a lot of _____ grease and a lot of trial and
PART OF THE BODY

_____ to build a boat that would actually _____
NOUN VERB

on top of the water! First he tried building his boat using some old

_____, a/an _____ _____-wacker and
PLURAL NOUN ADJECTIVE NOUN

a/an _____ plastic _____ from his yard. But that
COLOR ANIMAL

didn't work! Then he tied _____-gallon _____
NUMBER TYPE OF LIQUID

drums to a/an _____ mattress and set sail for the
ADJECTIVE

_____ seas, proving that if at first you don't succeed,
ADJECTIVE

_____ and _____ again! _____, from
VERB SAME VERB ADVERB

here on out, it will be smooth _____ for Captain Sumo!
VERB ENDING IN "ING"

From CLARENCE MAD LIBS® • TM & © Cartoon Network (s16). Published by Price Stern Sloan,
an imprint of Penguin Random House LLC, 345 Hudson Street, New York, NY 10014.

MAD LIBS® is fun to play with friends, but you can also play it by yourself! To begin with, DO NOT look at the story on the page below. Fill in the blanks on this page with the words called for. Then, using the words you have selected, fill in the blank spaces in the story.

Now you've created your own hilarious MAD LIBS® game!

CLARENCE'S SLEEPOVER INVITATION

VERB _____

ADJECTIVE _____

ADJECTIVE _____

VERB _____

A PLACE _____

PLURAL NOUN _____

NUMBER _____

TYPE OF FOOD _____

ANIMAL _____

NOUN _____

PART OF THE BODY (PLURAL) _____

COLOR _____

VERB _____

ADJECTIVE _____

ANIMAL (PLURAL) _____

EXCLAMATION _____

ADJECTIVE _____

MAD LIBS
CLARENCE'S SLEEPOVER INVITATION

Clarence is having a/an _____-over extravaganza, and you're
                        VERB

invited! Here are all the _____ details . . .
                            ADJECTIVE

Want to have the most _____ night of your life?
                         ADJECTIVE

_____ your way to (the) _____ for a night of fun
   VERB   A PLACE

and _____. First, we'll eat, like, _____ million
      PLURAL NOUN   NUMBER

_____ poppers. Then we'll play whack-a/an-_____,
 TYPE OF FOOD   ANIMAL

or crawl around in my secret _____! If that gets boring,
                                 NOUN

we can paint all ten of our _____ _____
                            PART OF THE BODY (PLURAL)   COLOR

and dress up like rock-and-_____ singers while we listen
                               VERB

to _____-metal music! Then we'll break open my mystery
    ADJECTIVE

piñata, which is filled with honey _____! _____!
                                    ANIMAL (PLURAL)   EXCLAMATION

This sleepover is going to be so _____!
                                    ADJECTIVE

From CLARENCE MAD LIBS® • TM & © Cartoon Network (s16). Published by Price Stern Sloan,
an imprint of Penguin Random House LLC, 345 Hudson Street, New York, NY 10014.

MAD LIBS® is fun to play with friends, but you can also play it by yourself! To begin with, DO NOT look at the story on the page below. Fill in the blanks on this page with the words called for. Then, using the words you have selected, fill in the blank spaces in the story.

Now you've created your own hilarious MAD LIBS® game!

PERSONAL HYGIENE, BY JEFF

PLURAL NOUN _____

NUMBER _____

ADJECTIVE _____

NOUN _____

PERSON IN ROOM _____

PART OF THE BODY _____

NOUN _____

ANIMAL (PLURAL) _____

ADVERB _____

PART OF THE BODY _____

VERB _____

A PLACE _____

NUMBER _____

TYPE OF FOOD (PLURAL) _____

NOUN _____

ADJECTIVE _____

MAD LIBS
PERSONAL HYGIENE,
BY JEFF

If you want to stay healthy, follow these four simple _____:
<u>PLURAL NOUN</u>

1. Shower at least _____ times a day using extremely
<u>NUMBER</u>

_____ water and plenty of antibacterial _____.
<u>ADJECTIVE</u> <u>NOUN</u>

2. Don't let anyone touch you, especially _____! Even
<u>PERSON IN ROOM</u>

a friendly _____-shake can expose you to millions of
<u>PART OF THE BODY</u>

potentially _____-threatening _____.
<u>NOUN</u> <u>ANIMAL (PLURAL)</u>

3. If someone does touch you, _____ use _____
<u>ADVERB</u> <u>PART OF THE BODY</u>

sanitizer to _____ the bacteria. Otherwise, you're
<u>VERB</u>

sure to end up in (the) _____ with a/an _____-
<u>A PLACE</u> <u>NUMBER</u>

degree fever!

4. Never, ever share your french _____, even if
<u>TYPE OF FOOD (PLURAL)</u>

Clarence begs you as if his _____ depended on it!
<u>NOUN</u>

His hands are totally _____!
<u>ADJECTIVE</u>

MAD LIBS® is fun to play with friends, but you can also play it by yourself! To begin with, DO NOT look at the story on the page below. Fill in the blanks on this page with the words called for. Then, using the words you have selected, fill in the blank spaces in the story.

Now you've created your own hilarious MAD LIBS® game!

CLARENCE'S COMEDY SCHOOL

CELEBRITY _____

OCCUPATION (PLURAL) _____

VERB _____

NOUN _____

NOUN _____

PLURAL NOUN _____

ANIMAL (PLURAL) _____

LAST NAME _____

VERB ENDING IN "ING" _____

ADJECTIVE _____

PLURAL NOUN _____

ADJECTIVE _____

NOUN _____

A PLACE _____

VERB _____

SILLY WORD _____

SAME SILLY WORD _____

MAD LIBS®
CLARENCE'S COMEDY SCHOOL

HONK! Do you want to be as funny as _____ or any of
<small>CELEBRITY</small>

Hollywood's other hysterically funny _____? Then
<small>OCCUPATION (PLURAL)</small>

_____ on down to your nearest _____ store
<small>VERB</small>   <small>NOUN</small>

and buy yourself a bicycle _____. *HONK!* Having a
<small>NOUN</small>

horn is guaranteed to make the _____ in your class laugh
<small>PLURAL NOUN</small>

like a bunch of _____. It even works on teachers, like
<small>ANIMAL (PLURAL)</small>

Ms. _____! *HONK!* You never need to worry about
<small>LAST NAME</small>

_____ your horn too much! Blowing a horn never gets
<small>VERB ENDING IN "ING"</small>

_____ or annoying! *HONK!* Also, don't forget to name your
<small>ADJECTIVE</small>

horn something funny like _____, so everyone knows how
<small>PLURAL NOUN</small>

_____ your horn is! *HONK! HONK!* Who knows? You may
<small>ADJECTIVE</small>

even get every _____ in (the) _____ to buy a horn
<small>NOUN</small>   <small>A PLACE</small>

and _____ them all at once like they're part of a student
<small>VERB</small>

orchestra! _____! _____!
<small>SILLY WORD</small>   <small>SAME SILLY WORD</small>

MAD LIBS® is fun to play with friends, but you can also play it by yourself! To begin with, DO NOT look at the story on the page below. Fill in the blanks on this page with the words called for. Then, using the words you have selected, fill in the blank spaces in the story.

Now you've created your own hilarious MAD LIBS® game!

GROSS-OUT STORIES

PLURAL NOUN _____

ADJECTIVE _____

CELEBRITY (FEMALE) _____

NOUN _____

ADJECTIVE _____

ADJECTIVE _____

VERB ENDING IN "ING" _____

ANIMAL _____

NOUN _____

TYPE OF LIQUID _____

PART OF THE BODY (PLURAL) _____

VEHICLE _____

TYPE OF FOOD _____

EXCLAMATION _____

PERSON IN ROOM (MALE) _____

PART OF THE BODY _____

VERB (PAST TENSE) _____

VERB _____

MAD LIBS

GROSS-OUT STORIES

Clarence and his guy _____ love to top each other with gross-
                          PLURAL NOUN

out stories, and they have some really _____ stories to tell.
                                            ADJECTIVE

But when _____ climbs up to their _____ house,
         CELEBRITY (FEMALE)   NOUN

they have a/an _____-out contest to see who is the most
                  ADJECTIVE

_____. Clarence told a story about _____ a
   ADJECTIVE   VERB ENDING IN "ING"

rotten _____ egg! Jeff told a story about when the shower
           ANIMAL

_____ got clogged, and dirty _____ almost
    NOUN   TYPE OF LIQUID

touched his _____! And Sumo told a story about
            PART OF THE BODY (PLURAL)

when his family took a road trip in a/an _____ and ate bad
                                             VEHICLE

clam _____. _____! But none of the stories could
     TYPE OF FOOD   EXCLAMATION

top when _____ got a kiss on the _____
         PERSON IN ROOM (MALE)   PART OF THE BODY

from Chelsea! *Ewwwww!* That's when everyone _____
                                              VERB (PAST TENSE)

out of the tree house so they could _____ up!
                                         VERB

From CLARENCE MAD LIBS® • TM & © Cartoon Network (s16). Published by Price Stern Sloan,
an imprint of Penguin Random House LLC, 345 Hudson Street, New York, NY 10014.

MAD LIBS® is fun to play with friends, but you can also play it by yourself! To begin with, DO NOT look at the story on the page below. Fill in the blanks on this page with the words called for. Then, using the words you have selected, fill in the blank spaces in the story.

Now you've created your own hilarious MAD LIBS® game!

BELSON'S PRANKS

PLURAL NOUN _____

VERB ENDING IN "ING" _____

PART OF THE BODY _____

NOUN _____

VERB ENDING IN "ING" _____

VERB _____

ADVERB _____

NUMBER _____

NOUN _____

NOUN _____

ADJECTIVE _____

NOUN _____

ARTICLE OF CLOTHING _____

PART OF THE BODY _____

PERSON IN ROOM (MALE) _____

ARTICLE OF CLOTHING _____

MAD LIBS®

BELSON'S PRANKS

Belson knows tons of practical _____ and loves to prank his
                                    PLURAL NOUN

friends! He starts with simple pranks, like _____ the
                                            VERB ENDING IN "ING"

cap off the saltshaker, or tickling Clarence's _____ with a/an
                                                PART OF THE BODY

_____ after putting _____ cream in his hand!
     NOUN   VERB ENDING IN "ING"

But if these pranks don't _____ very well, he _____
                              VERB   ADVERB

moves on to phase _____ of his master _____—
                       NUMBER   NOUN

pretending to be a serial _____ and chasing his friends around
                              NOUN

with a/an _____ _____-saw, while wearing a
           ADJECTIVE   NOUN

hockey _____ on his _____! Eventually, Sumo
       ARTICLE OF CLOTHING   PART OF THE BODY

figured out Belson's plan, but not before _____ had to
                                          PERSON IN ROOM (MALE)

put on Belson's mom's _____!
                      ARTICLE OF CLOTHING

From CLARENCE MAD LIBS® • TM & © Cartoon Network (s16). Published by Price Stern Sloan,
an imprint of Penguin Random House LLC, 345 Hudson Street, New York, NY 10014.

MAD LIBS® is fun to play with friends, but you can also play it by yourself! To begin with, DO NOT look at the story on the page below. Fill in the blanks on this page with the words called for. Then, using the words you have selected, fill in the blank spaces in the story.

Now you've created your own hilarious MAD LIBS® game!

THE DANGERS OF CLARENCE DOLLARS

PERSON IN ROOM _____

A PLACE _____

NOUN _____

PLURAL NOUN _____

VERB (PAST TENSE) _____

ADJECTIVE _____

PART OF THE BODY _____

SILLY WORD _____

PLURAL NOUN _____

TYPE OF FOOD _____

ADJECTIVE _____

VERB ENDING IN "ING" _____

PLURAL NOUN _____

VERB _____

VERB (PAST TENSE) _____

NOUN _____

MAD LIBS
THE DANGERS OF CLARENCE DOLLARS

_____ Dollars are one of the most powerful forces in
PERSON IN ROOM

(the) _____, right behind _____-quakes or
      A PLACE   NOUN

tidal _____. Clarence _____ this lesson the
      PLURAL NOUN   VERB (PAST TENSE)

_____ way when he made his own money by drawing
ADJECTIVE

his _____ on a piece of paper. At first, everyone at
    PART OF THE BODY

_____ Elementary thought Clarence _____
SILLY WORD   PLURAL NOUN

were the best idea since sliced _____. But when the
                                 TYPE OF FOOD

demand for his dollars got too _____, and students started
                                ADJECTIVE

_____ each other and throwing _____ at
VERB ENDING IN "ING"   PLURAL NOUN

Ms. Baker, Clarence had to _____ the market to keep the
                            VERB

school from being _____ to the ground! Maybe the Buddy
                  VERB (PAST TENSE)

_____ system isn't so bad, after all.
NOUN

From CLARENCE MAD LIBS® • TM & © Cartoon Network (s16). Published by Price Stern Sloan,
an imprint of Penguin Random House LLC, 345 Hudson Street, New York, NY 10014.

MAD LIBS® is fun to play with friends, but you can also play it by yourself! To begin with, DO NOT look at the story on the page below. Fill in the blanks on this page with the words called for. Then, using the words you have selected, fill in the blank spaces in the story.

Now you've created your own hilarious MAD LIBS® game!

GIRL SLUMBER PARTY SURPRISE!

ANIMAL (PLURAL) _____

NOUN _____

NOUN _____

VERB _____

EXCLAMATION _____

VERB _____

PLURAL NOUN _____

SILLY WORD _____

PART OF THE BODY _____

ANIMAL _____

NUMBER _____

VERB _____

ADJECTIVE _____

NOUN _____

PART OF THE BODY (PLURAL) _____

PERSON IN ROOM (MALE) _____

VERB (PAST TENSE) _____

VERB ENDING IN "ING" _____

MAD LIBS®
GIRL SLUMBER PARTY SURPRISE!

When Clarence arrived covered in gummy _____ at
                                        ANIMAL (PLURAL)

a/an _____ slumber party, he was afraid he had just made
         NOUN

the biggest _____ of his life! After all, he thought he was
                 NOUN

going to a boys' _____-over! _____! But he
                      VERB   EXCLAMATION

soon discovered that the girls didn't just want to _____
                                                         VERB

to music by Kids to _____, put Razzle-_____
                       PLURAL NOUN   SILLY WORD

_____ gel in their hair, or watch the movie
PART OF THE BODY

Were-_____ *Boyfriend* _____ over and over. They
          ANIMAL   NUMBER

also wanted to _____ toilet paper into the trees, smash a/an
                     VERB

_____ gnome under the light of the full _____,
   ADJECTIVE   NOUN

and make gummy-worm _____ just like he did! By
                         PART OF THE BODY (PLURAL)

the end of the night, _____ had so much fun, he
                         PERSON IN ROOM (MALE)

almost _____ his pants! It turns out, girl slumber parties
         VERB (PAST TENSE)

are totally mind-_____!
                   VERB ENDING IN "ING"

MAD LIBS® is fun to play with friends, but you can also play it by yourself! To begin with, DO NOT look at the story on the page below. Fill in the blanks on this page with the words called for. Then, using the words you have selected, fill in the blank spaces in the story.

Now you've created your own hilarious MAD LIBS® game!

CHAD'S GUIDE TO LIFE

PLURAL NOUN _____

ADJECTIVE _____

ADJECTIVE _____

NOUN _____

ADJECTIVE _____

TYPE OF FOOD _____

PART OF THE BODY (PLURAL) _____

VEHICLE _____

LETTER OF THE ALPHABET _____

PLURAL NOUN _____

NOUN _____

NOUN _____

TYPE OF FOOD (PLURAL) _____

VERB _____

MAD LIBS

CHAD'S GUIDE TO LIFE

Chad knows that life's little _____ aren't worth getting upset
                                 PLURAL NOUN

about! After all, life is never _____! So when Chad has a/an
                                  ADJECTIVE

_____ problem, he doesn't freak out about it! For example, if
  ADJECTIVE

Clarence falls through the dining room _____ at his friend's
                                            NOUN

_____ dinner party, Chad just ignores it. And if Clarence
  ADJECTIVE

wrecks the house by using a/an _____ as a bowling ball,
                                 TYPE OF FOOD

Chad just shrugs his _____. It takes a lot to upset
                      PART OF THE BODY (PLURAL)

Chad, especially if he's watching *Monster* _____ *Jousting* on
                                              VEHICLE

TV. In fact, the only time Chad ever got upset was when he forgot

his _____-IP backstage _____ to see Rake
    LETTER OF THE ALPHABET   PLURAL NOUN

_____-burn! But that was only because the tickets were a/an
  NOUN

_____ for Mary. So follow Chad's example, and remember,
  NOUN

if life gives you _____, _____ lemonade!
                  TYPE OF FOOD (PLURAL)   VERB

From CLARENCE MAD LIBS® • TM & © Cartoon Network (s16). Published by Price Stern Sloan,
an imprint of Penguin Random House LLC, 345 Hudson Street, New York, NY 10014.

MAD LIBS® is fun to play with friends, but you can also play it by yourself! To begin with, DO NOT look at the story on the page below. Fill in the blanks on this page with the words called for. Then, using the words you have selected, fill in the blank spaces in the story.

Now you've created your own hilarious MAD LIBS® game!

UNTAMED VIDEO GAMES!

PLURAL NOUN _____

VERB _____

NUMBER _____

ADVERB _____

ADJECTIVE _____

TYPE OF LIQUID _____

PLURAL NOUN _____

NOUN _____

LETTER OF THE ALPHABET _____

VERB _____

ADJECTIVE _____

ARTICLE OF CLOTHING _____

VERB _____

NOUN _____

ADJECTIVE _____

EXCLAMATION _____

VERB ENDING IN "ING" _____

MAD LIBS®

UNTAMED VIDEO GAMES!

Video _____ are the best! Clarence and his friends love to
           PLURAL NOUN

_____ them all the time. The Acedia _____
    VERB   NUMBER

system (_____ not available in the United States until next
              ADVERB

year) has _____ games like *Psychopathic Ice-_____*
           ADJECTIVE   TYPE OF LIQUID

Man! In that game, the player shoots innocent _____ with
                                                    PLURAL NOUN

_____-cream cones. No wonder it's rated _____
   NOUN   LETTER OF THE ALPHABET

for *insane*! But no system can compare to Cerebrus _____!
                                                         VERB

That system comes with a/an _____ helmet and an
                                  ADJECTIVE

electronic _____ that the player uses to _____
           ARTICLE OF CLOTHING   VERB

the action! Some of the Cerebrus Breach games, like _____
                                                         NOUN

Planner 3000, are so _____, they don't even have levels!
                            ADJECTIVE

_____! Just don't get too addicted to them, or you'll end up
   EXCLAMATION

_____ standing up!
VERB ENDING IN "ING"

MAD LIBS® is fun to play with friends, but you can also play it by yourself! To begin with, DO NOT look at the story on the page below. Fill in the blanks on this page with the words called for. Then, using the words you have selected, fill in the blank spaces in the story.

Now you've created your own hilarious MAD LIBS® game!

WHY MOMS ARE GREAT

ADJECTIVE _____

PERSON IN ROOM (FEMALE) _____

COLOR _____

ARTICLE OF CLOTHING (PLURAL) _____

ADJECTIVE _____

VERB ENDING IN "ING" _____

NOUN _____

PLURAL NOUN _____

ADJECTIVE _____

TYPE OF FOOD _____

NOUN _____

PART OF THE BODY _____

ADJECTIVE _____

NOUN _____

ADJECTIVE _____

PLURAL NOUN _____

PLURAL NOUN _____

WHY MOMS ARE GREAT

Moms are so _____! Especially Clarence's mom,
ADJECTIVE

_____ Wendell. She's got _____ hair,
PERSON IN ROOM (FEMALE)   COLOR

wears tight pink _____, and talks with a really
ARTICLE OF CLOTHING (PLURAL)

_____ accent. She's always _____ what's best
ADJECTIVE   VERB ENDING IN "ING"

for her _____. She clips _____ to save money
NOUN   PLURAL NOUN

on groceries, always buys _____ fruit, and makes the best
ADJECTIVE

_____ salad ever! Mary loves Clarence more than her own
TYPE OF FOOD

_____ and wants to give him anything his _____
NOUN   PART OF THE BODY

desires. But that doesn't mean she spoils him _____!
ADJECTIVE

If she did, Clarence could end up like Belson, who's a real spoiled

_____. Instead, she gives Clarence what he needs most—
NOUN

lots of _____ encouragement, tons of _____, and
ADJECTIVE   PLURAL NOUN

dozens of big, warm _____!
PLURAL NOUN

From CLARENCE MAD LIBS® • TM & © Cartoon Network (s16). Published by Price Stern Sloan,
an imprint of Penguin Random House LLC, 345 Hudson Street, New York, NY 10014.

MAD LIBS® is fun to play with friends, but you can also play it by yourself! To begin with, DO NOT look at the story on the page below. Fill in the blanks on this page with the words called for. Then, using the words you have selected, fill in the blank spaces in the story.

Now you've created your own hilarious MAD LIBS® game!

TO FIB OR NOT TO FIB

VERB _____

ADVERB _____

ADJECTIVE _____

VERB ENDING IN "ING" _____

ADJECTIVE _____

ANIMAL _____

NOUN _____

VERB (PAST TENSE) _____

NUMBER _____

NOUN _____

PLURAL NOUN _____

ANIMAL (PLURAL) _____

ADJECTIVE _____

VERB _____

ADJECTIVE _____

NOUN _____

MAD☺LIBS®

TO FIB OR NOT TO FIB

Sometimes Clarence has a hard time knowing when to

_____the truth! Like when he _____ broke Jeff's
　　　　VERB　　　　　　　　　　　　　　　ADVERB

brand-_____ toy, the _____ Wrath Hover
　　　　ADJECTIVE　　　　　　　VERB ENDING IN "ING"

Ginsbot! To avoid making Jeff really _____, Clarence told
　　　　　　　　　　　　　　　　　ADJECTIVE

him that a/an _____ broke into Jeff's _____
　　　　　　　　ANIMAL　　　　　　　　　　　　　NOUN

and _____ the toy into _____ pieces. Clarence
　　　VERB (PAST TENSE)　　　　　　NUMBER

said the raccoon then tried to fix the flying _____,
　　　　　　　　　　　　　　　　　　　　　　　NOUN

but that she couldn't because raccoons can't fix _____
　　　　　　　　　　　　　　　　　　　　　　PLURAL NOUN

like _____ can! There was no way that someone as
　　ANIMAL (PLURAL)

_____ as Jeff would _____ that _____
　ADJECTIVE　　　　　　　　VERB　　　　　　　ADJECTIVE

story, so Sumo told Jeff the truth! It turns out honesty is the best

_____ after all!
　　NOUN

From CLARENCE MAD LIBS® • TM & © Cartoon Network (s16). Published by Price Stern Sloan,
an imprint of Penguin Random House LLC, 345 Hudson Street, New York, NY 10014.

MAD LIBS® is fun to play with friends, but you can also play it by yourself! To begin with, DO NOT look at the story on the page below. Fill in the blanks on this page with the words called for. Then, using the words you have selected, fill in the blank spaces in the story.

Now you've created your own hilarious MAD LIBS® game!

HOW TO WIN AT THE PIZZA SWAMP

PLURAL NOUN _____

A PLACE _____

ADJECTIVE _____

TYPE OF FOOD _____

NOUN _____

ADJECTIVE _____

PART OF THE BODY (PLURAL) _____

ANIMAL (PLURAL) _____

NOUN _____

VERB ENDING IN "ING" _____

NOUN _____

PLURAL NOUN _____

NOUN _____

PLURAL NOUN _____

PLURAL NOUN _____

NOUN _____

OCCUPATION _____

MAD LIBS®
HOW TO WIN AT THE
PIZZA SWAMP

If you want to win _____ at the Pizza _____,
PLURAL NOUN   A PLACE

you'll need to know these _____ game strategies:
ADJECTIVE

1. Keep your energy up by eating other people's _____
TYPE OF FOOD

   crusts and leftover birthday _____. Gaming is
   NOUN

   _____ work!
   ADJECTIVE

2. To win at Seal Whack, use your _____ to hit the
   PART OF THE BODY (PLURAL)

   _____ instead of using the rubber _____.
   ANIMAL (PLURAL)   NOUN

3. When _____ laser tag, you can use a disco
   VERB ENDING IN "ING"

   _____ to refract red _____ all over the
   NOUN   PLURAL NOUN

   place, and beat the dreaded _____ ghost!
   NOUN

4. When playing Money Broom, try to beat the _____
   PLURAL NOUN

   by calculating how often the machine spits out _____.
   PLURAL NOUN

5. Never underestimate the power of a Wizard _____!
   NOUN

   _____ Dollars are magical!
   OCCUPATION

From CLARENCE MAD LIBS® • TM & © Cartoon Network (s16). Published by Price Stern Sloan,
an imprint of Penguin Random House LLC, 345 Hudson Street, New York, NY 10014.

MAD LIBS® is fun to play with friends, but you can also play it by yourself! To begin with, DO NOT look at the story on the page below. Fill in the blanks on this page with the words called for. Then, using the words you have selected, fill in the blank spaces in the story.

Now you've created your own hilarious MAD LIBS® game!

CLARENCE'S DAY PLANNER

NOUN _____

ADJECTIVE _____

VERB _____

VERB _____

NOUN _____

ADJECTIVE _____

NOUN _____

NOUN _____

VERB _____

PLURAL NOUN _____

EXCLAMATION _____

PART OF THE BODY _____

TYPE OF FOOD _____

VERB ENDING IN "ING" _____

ADJECTIVE _____

ANIMAL _____

A PLACE _____

ADJECTIVE _____

MAD LIBS

CLARENCE'S DAY PLANNER

Clarence wakes up way before the _____ rises. Mostly
                                        NOUN

because the sun is a/an _____-bones! Here's a page from his
                              ADJECTIVE

day planner:

- 5:00 a.m.: Get up and _____ out. Make your muscles
                                VERB

  _____ like they are on _____!
       VERB   NOUN

- 5:06 a.m.: Clean the _____ floors by riding around on a
                              ADJECTIVE

  robot _____.
            NOUN

- 5:14 a.m.: Use a/an _____ machine to go back in time and
                            NOUN

  _____ prehistoric _____. _____!
       VERB   PLURAL NOUN   EXCLAMATION

- 5:21 a.m.: Pretend to shave your _____ using whipped
                                        PART OF THE BODY

  _____ instead of _____ cream.
     TYPE OF FOOD   VERB ENDING IN "ING"

- 6:36 a.m.: Protect _____ raccoons from an angry
                            ADJECTIVE

  mountain _____.
                ANIMAL

- 7:00 a.m.: Go to school at (the) _____ and have
                                        A PLACE

  a/an _____ day!
         ADJECTIVE

MAD LIBS® is fun to play with friends, but you can also play it by yourself! To begin with, DO NOT look at the story on the page below. Fill in the blanks on this page with the words called for. Then, using the words you have selected, fill in the blank spaces in the story.

Now you've created your own hilarious MAD LIBS® game!

ROUGH RIDERS CHICKEN'S "SPECIAL" SAUCE

ADJECTIVE _____

ANIMAL _____

ADJECTIVE _____

NOUN _____

ADJECTIVE _____

NOUN _____

TYPE OF LIQUID _____

PART OF THE BODY _____

VERB ENDING IN "ING" _____

PERSON IN ROOM _____

VERB (PAST TENSE) _____

ANIMAL _____

ADVERB _____

NOUN _____

CELEBRITY (MALE) _____

CELEBRITY (FEMALE) _____

VERB (PAST TENSE) _____

EXCLAMATION _____

MAD☺LIBS
ROUGH RIDERS CHICKEN'S
"SPECIAL" SAUCE

When _____ Riders Chicken introduced a new sauce for
            ADJECTIVE

their _____ nuggets at Aberdale Elementary, Clarence
            ANIMAL

had a vision of the future! And it wasn't _____! First the
                                              ADJECTIVE

whole _____ became obsessed with the _____
            NOUN   ADJECTIVE

taste of the new cinnamon _____ sauce, but it turned out
                                  NOUN

the special _____ was actually used for _____
                TYPE OF LIQUID   PART OF THE BODY

control! With everyone _____ like crazed zombies,
                            VERB ENDING IN "ING"

including _____, Clarence had to save Sumo from being
                PERSON IN ROOM

_____ into an alien _____. _____,
VERB (PAST TENSE)   ANIMAL   ADVERB

Rake Backburn showed up just in the nick of _____ with
                                                    NOUN

_____ and _____, and they _____
CELEBRITY (MALE)   CELEBRITY (FEMALE)   VERB (PAST TENSE)

up the school with dynamite before Sumo could say, *"Cluck! Cluck!"*

_____!
EXCLAMATION

From CLARENCE MAD LIBS® • TM & © Cartoon Network (s16). Published by Price Stern Sloan,
an imprint of Penguin Random House LLC, 345 Hudson Street, New York, NY 10014.

MAD LIBS® is fun to play with friends, but you can also play it by yourself! To begin with, DO NOT look at the story on the page below. Fill in the blanks on this page with the words called for. Then, using the words you have selected, fill in the blank spaces in the story.

Now you've created your own hilarious MAD LIBS® game!

BOOBY TRAPS FOR BURGERS

TYPE OF FOOD (PLURAL) _____

A PLACE (PLURAL) _____

NOUN _____

PERSON IN ROOM (MALE) _____

VERB _____

PLURAL NOUN _____

SILLY WORD _____

TYPE OF FOOD (PLURAL) _____

ADJECTIVE _____

SILLY WORD _____

PLURAL NOUN _____

PART OF THE BODY _____

NOUN _____

TYPE OF LIQUID _____

PART OF THE BODY _____

PART OF THE BODY _____

MAD LIBS®

BOOBY TRAPS FOR BURGERS

Burglars (or _____, as Clarence calls them) are a
_____TYPE OF FOOD (PLURAL)_____

threat to suburban _____ everywhere! So when Clarence's
_____A PLACE (PLURAL)_____

mom and her _____-friend, _____, leave
_____NOUN_____ ____PERSON IN ROOM (MALE)____

Clarence home alone with Jeff and Sumo, Clarence puts the house on

maximum _____-down! First, they use all the food in the
_____VERB_____

_____ to make _____ traps. For example, they
___PLURAL NOUN___ ____SILLY WORD____

put slippery _____ on the floor to slide _____
_____TYPE OF FOOD (PLURAL)_____ _____ADJECTIVE_____

"burgers" out the window. Pasta la _____, baby! But
_____SILLY WORD_____

when Chad arrives home early, they have to trigger the booby

_____themselves. Jeff gets hit in the _____ with
___PLURAL NOUN___ ____PART OF THE BODY____

hot _____ powder, and Sumo gets tomato _____
_____NOUN_____ _____TYPE OF LIQUID_____

dumped on his _____. Fortunately Chad gets out alive, but
____PART OF THE BODY____

only by the skin of his _____!
_____PART OF THE BODY_____

From CLARENCE MAD LIBS® • TM & © Cartoon Network (s16). Published by Price Stern Sloan,
an imprint of Penguin Random House LLC, 345 Hudson Street, New York, NY 10014.

MAD LIBS® is fun to play with friends, but you can also play it by yourself! To begin with, DO NOT look at the story on the page below. Fill in the blanks on this page with the words called for. Then, using the words you have selected, fill in the blank spaces in the story.

Now you've created your own hilarious MAD LIBS® game!

NATURE KATE IS GREAT

PERSON IN ROOM (FEMALE) _____

OCCUPATION _____

ADJECTIVE _____

ANIMAL _____

PART OF THE BODY (PLURAL) _____

NOUN _____

PERSON IN ROOM (MALE) _____

PLURAL NOUN _____

VEHICLE _____

ADJECTIVE _____

ANIMAL _____

PART OF THE BODY (PLURAL) _____

NOUN _____

VERB ENDING IN "ING" _____

ADJECTIVE _____

ADVERB _____

NOUN _____

MAD LIBS

NATURE KATE IS GREAT

Nature _____ is the bravest _____
      PERSON IN ROOM (FEMALE)   OCCUPATION

to ever work inside a state park! Kate is so _____, she
                                         ADJECTIVE

once saved Clarence from being bitten by a rattle-_____
                                           ANIMAL

using only her bare _____, and then floated him
                        PART OF THE BODY (PLURAL)

to safety using her own para-_____. Or at least that's
                               NOUN

what _____ says. He tends to exaggerate his
        PERSON IN ROOM (MALE)

_____. Either way, Nature Kate definitely rescued Sumo
PLURAL NOUN

from being lost after he escaped from Josh's _____ in the
                                      VEHICLE

_____ desert. And she rescued Clarence and his friends
ADJECTIVE

near _____'s Bridge when their attempts to link their
     ANIMAL

hands and _____ together to make a human
           PART OF THE BODY (PLURAL)

_____ failed to save Josh from _____ off a
NOUN   VERB ENDING IN "ING"

cliff. For _____ Kate, being _____ brave is just
        ADJECTIVE   ADVERB

part of being a park _____!
             NOUN

From CLARENCE MAD LIBS® • TM & © Cartoon Network (s16). Published by Price Stern Sloan, an imprint of Penguin Random House LLC, 345 Hudson Street, New York, NY 10014.

MAD LIBS® is fun to play with friends, but you can also play it by yourself! To begin with, DO NOT look at the story on the page below. Fill in the blanks on this page with the words called for. Then, using the words you have selected, fill in the blank spaces in the story.

Now you've created your own hilarious MAD LIBS® game!

CLARENCE'S PHILOSOPHY ON LIFE!

NOUN _____

ADJECTIVE _____

ADVERB _____

NOUN _____

ADJECTIVE _____

CELEBRITY _____

ANIMAL _____

PART OF THE BODY _____

ADJECTIVE _____

NOUN _____

ADJECTIVE _____

PLURAL NOUN _____

PART OF THE BODY _____

PLURAL NOUN _____

NOUN _____

MAD LIBS
CLARENCE'S PHILOSOPHY ON LIFE!

Clarence can make even the most boring _____ more fun
                                              NOUN
than anyone could have ever imagined. And it's all because of his

_____ attitude—the way he _____ savors every
   ADJECTIVE   ADVERB
_____ in life, and because he's _____ to everyone
   NOUN   ADJECTIVE
and everything he meets, no matter if they're a famous TV star like

_____ or just a lowly earth-_____ wiggling around
   CELEBRITY   ANIMAL
in the mud with no _____. Clarence knows that with
                     PART OF THE BODY
a/an _____ attitude, even getting lost in the _____
        ADJECTIVE   NOUN
underneath the city streets can be the most _____ day of
                                                ADJECTIVE
your life! Clarence treats his friends like _____, and always
                                               PLURAL NOUN
makes decisions based on how he feels in his _____. Given
                                                PART OF THE BODY
all these great personality _____, it's easy to see how Clarence
                               PLURAL NOUN
has truly discovered the _____ to happiness!
                            NOUN

Download Mad Libs today!

Join the millions of Mad Libs fans creating
wacky and wonderful stories on our apps!